FRETS & STRUTS

FRETS & STRUTS

Poems by
Barry Spacks

Copyright © 2014 Barry Spacks

Word Palace Press
P.O. Box 583
San Luis Obispo, CA 93406
wordpalacepress.com
wordpalacepress@aol.com

Book and Cover Design By
    S. Garrett Stotko

ISBN: 0-9888045-5-7
ISBN-13: 978-0-9888045-5-5

ACKNOWLEDGEMENTS:

With thanks to the editors of the following journals, in which various of these poems first appeared, some in earlier forms:

ART LIFE, ASKEW, BROKEN PLATE, CALIFORNIA QUARTERLY, FOLLY, HOPKINS REVIEW, INNISFREE POETRY REVIEW, INTO THE TEETH OF THE WIND, IRONWOOD, MOCKINGBIRD, NEW ORLEANS REVIEW, OAK BEND REVIEW, POETRY NORTHWEST, RED OCHRE, ROCK SPRINGS, SEWANEE REVIEW, SOLO CAFE, SALT RIVER REVIEW, SOTTO VOCE, SPECTRUM, SPIRITUALITY & HEALTH, STAND, TAR RIVER POETRY, TATTOO HIGHWAY, THE LABLETTER, THE TORONTO QUARTERLY, THE VIEW FROM HERE, THRUSH POETRY JOURNAL, UMBRELLA, UNDERGROUND VOICES, VERSE WISCONSIN and X-CONNECT

Contents

I.

WOMEN ON MEN 3
WHAT IS A POET? 4
SHE TO HIM, HE TO HER 5
A CHOOSING 6
LOVE POEM 7
THOSE BILLIONS 8
LOST & FOUND 9
TO THE DELICATE GIRL WHO SAT BESIDE ME ON A CROWDED BUS 10
ON A LINE FROM HENNY YOUNGMAN 11
GIRL-BIRD 12
SHIRLEY 13
A THICK BOOK 14
SONG OF THE WOODEN MAN 15
DEFINING EROS 16
A MOMENT WITH HEMINGWAY 19
STONEWORKERS 20
A GUINNESS 21

II.

GOOD OLD DREAMS
    23
THE HEAVINESS OF A STONE
    24
THE EDEN STORY
    25
WHY WOMEN LOVE GOOD SHOES
    26
HAPPINESS
    27
HAIRS
    28
BITCH-WANTS
    29
ALZ
    30
PASSENGER WONG
    31
SIXTEEN
    32
THE JUICE
    33
WALKING WITH THE POET TED MACKER
    34
JOLSON & LOUIE
    35
PIANISSIMO
    36
SONG: DESCENDING TO TOUCH
    37

for
(ever)
KIMBERLEY

I.

WOMEN ON MEN

my friend Chryss
writes about men:
too attentive, not attentive enough,

too serious, too frivolous

too this too that

till we weep with hilarity when she says
"I really feel sorry for them!"

and how her book should be entitled:
"Some Poems That Explain Why I'll Live Alone
for the Rest of My Life"

*

a woman's silent stare,
waiting for you to do something,
something RIGHT!

*

Rilke had ancestors tossing down coins
as applause from heaven for lovers who'd learned
to be acrobats of love, and soar.

WHAT IS A POET?

A poet is a pig for endorphins.
The beautiful world murmurs
"Do me some jazzy, Dollink,
whisper my name."

*

Poets are mainly reminders:
kin, in that way, to bears, orchids,
kindly deeds, obsessive loves...
worlds emergent from murmur -- TA-DA!

*

Muse, sweetheart, help me to speak
the winter-bowed sapling; the check-out girl's
monitored pain; the mountains in sunlight;
the mountain-top-moments of exaltation.

SHE TO HIM, HE TO HER

She to him is Silkiness;
Pleasure Dome;
Danger Zone.

He to her? Stubborn Stallion.
Oliver who whispers "More."
Phantom of the opera where he'd star.

May he be her Joyful Nuzzler;
Seedtree; Brilliant Midnight Totem;
Key to Spicechest; Totaled Column.

A CHOOSING

Reading my old pal Eudora's book,
her funny uncles, motorcar trips
from Jackson to West Virginia, the grandmother
writing Eudora's mother a letter
daily, then off down the mountain to post it,

somehow this brings back my childhood's particulars,
shoveling coal to our basement furnace,
the basement's wet dog smell, Dorothy Schectman
playing piano across the way
(a pure Eudora moment) — memory

flowing. Dorothy my first wife in childhood
who called from her porch one teen-time December
asking which would I take to some party,
she or her friend Shirley Scharf by her side,
and though I yearned for wild-girl Shirley

I honored the grown-ups' version, the Barry
& Dorothy show, chose Dorothy, answered
"You" as promptly as any husband,
refusing desertion, not knowing then
the theme of my life had been written in stone.

LOVE POEM

The small possum
I ran into face to face
in the back garden,
both of us shocked
by so sudden a meeting,

this dear-faced
innocent opossum who might next
have slipped inside the house,
brave as a raccoon,
after the cat's food,

I frightened him with my too loud
"Hello!" Oh, I tell you
I loved that little beastie
in a small way
for a small while.

THOSE BILLIONS

The great sage Soraya
after years of retreat
still hadn't "got it"

till he was told
to lie on the earth,
feel its firmness,

hear the now & then barking
of the monastery's dogs;
gaze at the stars, those billions

LOST & FOUND

Closing time, the bartender checks
for items left behind (Ray-Ban
shades...once a black runner's bra).
He gathers glasses with their dregs,

brooding, a poet, on how to describe
the beer-tang, dark-wood-smell of the place
which he knows will ripen once the sun
breathes on the louvers, wanting in.

The smell's like the ghost of an ongoing sound,
like the tang and sway of back-up singers
humming after the music's connivings
have dimmed. He feels invited now

to judge his life's improbable risks:
keys in hand he's thinking *damn*
at the run of his inventory of loss,
enduring a shuffle of inward snapshots:

lovers, friends, now distant or gone,
and no reprieve. The bar seems huge
and he's approaching something huge,
a place for the lost & found.

TO THE DELICATE GIRL WHO SAT BESIDE ME ON A CROWDED BUS

In deference to your delicacy
(How does one know such things? The shoulder knows)

I held to the seat-top on bus curves
not to lurch ungainly your way.

I read an old *New Yorker*, pretending
I failed to sense you beside me,

but came a bump at a turning you fell
against my arm. You felt like cream.

Later, at the end of our journey,
standing to leave, you halted -- it seemed

my leg had caught your gypsy skirt.
We laughed, of course, as I released you.

"Had you trapped a bit," I said,
and that was the end of our brief affair.

ON A LINE FROM HENNY YOUNGMAN
(*"When God sneezed, I didn't know what to say."*)

How to respond to God if She sneezes.
"Go bless Yourself"? Say something friendly,
for think how lonely She must be,

no one around for tennis or ping-pong,
no other Universe to make eyes at,
no Beyond beyond. Poor God,

forever She's stuck being everyone,
only Herself for arguments,
for blissed-out, naked afternoons.

No wonder, in Her goatly He-mode,
She drifts into all these rowdy affairs
with Leda, Europa, Mary. Likewise

Her ceaseless wonders and saxophones.
God-bless You, God, and all Your excesses --
Your dolphins, and sunsets, and Judy Garlands!

GIRL-BIRD

Tight at the shoulders, full at the breast,
ample below, that's a Girl-Bird, all right;
she's never met a cliff she wouldn't fly from.

Diamond-chips conspire in the depths
of her eyes: soul-lights flashing give-over,
for those are the words of the Girl-Bird's song.

*Give over, give over, you Boy Bird, it goes:
rise up this instant, you simplex-libido,
O, weave your wand, you silly member.*

This sexy sister preens her feathers.
What turns her into a comely woman
is anyone's guess: she feels the need

for spatulas, a nice herb garden,
wakes at noon to ponder ring-tones;
grounded, molts. Such an odd species,

fueled by the surge from the Girl-Bird core,
all sighs and zazz: everyone wants one,
thoughtfully rouging a lip, intent

at the racks, in line at the movies atilt
on a high-heel, hilarious, chatting with friends
as they wait their turn at the popcorn stand.

SHIRLEY

Shirley, this old elephant on the Nature special,
had lived completely alone for twenty years
cared for by a devoted keeper who washed her
and trimmed her nails,

but that's not the same as a companion elephant.
Elephants are herd-creatures like us,
so poor Shirley, who once worked in a circus,
it must have pained her, twenty years in solitude.

But after her circus years and the twenty lonely years
they sent her to an Elephant Pure Land,
a great good place in Tennessee
where they take in abused or saddened elephants,

and there she met an old friend from circus days
and they trumpeted and stroked each other
and they actually hugged with their trunks
and couldn't be separated forever and ever.

I thought in my yearly Valentine's poem
I might use this image of loving elephants
to please my dear wife, except it's tricky,
an elephant-reference can insult a lady.

A joke to us, but in Indian poetry
serious sexiness is meant
when Shiva feels stirred by slim Shakti and notes
that she moves in her walk "like an elephant."

To Shakti and Shiva, that delicate gait's
voluptuous: a dancerly sway
you can see at the zoo, or the circus parade,
or in some 3 a.m. reverie

A THICK BOOK

for Carol DeCanio

The way you talk about books: chapter heads,
covers, colophons -- taken-care!

And the smell of a book, the feel of its paper,
the heft of the thing...and of course the fonts

(plus the note in the back about the fonts)
and the plot, metaphors — all those words!

I tell you it beats praising nightingales,
it's almost as fine as cheering mail

to hear the way you go on about
"a thick book — with *pages* in it!"

SONG OF THE WOODEN MAN

after "The Jewel Mirror Samadhi"
by Ch'an Master Tung-shan Liang-chieh

Because there is the base
there is house, cat, cow;
jeweled pedestals;
fine clothing.

The stone woman offers up the dance;
the wooden man begins to sing.

Excitement? doubt? – both pitfalls,
for nothing comes nor goes:
path and traveler merging,
you are not it; it is actually you.

Hiding a heron in the moonlight;
filling a silver bowl with snow.

Yi with his archer's skill
strikes targets at hundreds of paces...
but arrow-heads meeting point-on? —
can this be caused by targeting?

The stone woman offers up the dance;
the wooden man begins to sing.

This is the host within the host:
a tethered horse, secretly whirling,
ecstatic rat, outwardly calm.
You have it now, so keep it well.

Hiding a heron in the moonlight;
filling a silver bowl with snow.

DEFINING EROS

Desire words of Rilke, Catullus, Rumi
lift the body toward delicacy
like the scent
before the savoring
of tea.

*

That naked girl in spectacles
reading Borges.

*

May pleasuring prevail.
May all dear bodies know full joy.

(Name one of us who'd not be touched all over).

*

The lover gains his bliss
 feeling what he feels she feels
to feel his hands, his lips.

*

How beautiful we were
with all our youth at play
not knowing then, despite our heat,
that we were burning

*

In the Golden Age
butterflies mated with humans.
From this came need for light landings
and yearnings to fly.

*

What is she trying to tell me
lightly traipsing from room to room
in nothing but tiny white socks?

*

The brain, vast sexual organ,
fed by fantasy, by images, yes,
for centuries
engorged by words.

*

mummy wrapped words of Sappho:

*may that shining girl
come to me*

*

Her beauty
beneath a gauzy blouse and skirt...

unclothed already she would be

the meaning
without its poem.

*

Seventeen, I worked for one day
door to door with a book of pictures,
supposed to sell refrigerators.

Insane. But a woman let me in
to sales-talk as she ironed, room
curtained, dim.

She already had a refrigerator.

For years I carried a sense of the musk
in that room,

too young, too much a salesman to see
               how much she'd wanted to give away.

A MOMENT WITH HEMINGWAY

Hemingway sits, blessed by hunger,
in a Gauloise cafe.

He remembers up in Michigan.

His pen moves on rough paper
over the scarred table
in a knowing way.

He has joined the surge
of the universe.

Sweet power of emotion
there in his body
seeks words to carry feeling through.

Out of genius, out of "fullness,"
a young man in Paris,
he writes his story "Three Day Blow."

What deeply happens
continues forever.

You were there once too
— remember?

STONEWORKERS

Sartre writes that all souls cry out
if you beat your soul...but you must go public.
Gag the poor thing in its feted cell
and you're comfortless, humming your dirge
"Why me? Why me the self-assassin?"

Tell us then how you seemed to be chosen
to slam your mind from wall to wall
while stoneworkers swagger home at night
(or so you think) for drink and sex
crying "Damn, but today we laid us some stone!"

A GUINNESS

Why, Lord, are women so beautiful?
Near Galway once in a pub I met
a bar-girl, Botticellian Venus,
blessedly clothed this time.

Nature takes no chances: storms
of sperm, ample provision made
to assure a replacement for Woody Allen,
the next generation's bar-girl.

She made me think of heart-seared heroes
blinded because they'd gazed on a Goddess,
this one who self-contentedly
drew me a Guinness.

II.

GOOD OLD DREAMS

These days I'm busy admiring dreaming.
Turns out I'm one of these athlete-dreamers
producing mind-movies, reading aloud
from a student's poem in a stadium
where the kids in the grandstand wildly applaud
line after line — I'm so proud of this girl
who wrote the thing, but wake to the fact
that I was the poem's "onlie begettor"
(who else? It's me clocks-in for dream time)
no need for revision, the biting of pencil,
self-doubt, come-ON! you can dream whole novels,
(once, with no sweat, an epic poem).

What if some cyber-device could print out
a DVD of such churning dreams?
A night-job! Making a living by sleep!
"Goodnight, Hon," we'd say, "we writers
must get to work," and there next day
would ease from the skull a masterpiece
with Amy Adams, costing millions
the Hollywood way but here for free,
plus also the dreamer achieves the sex-scenes,
he's everyone in the dream, the grips,
the whole Art Department, DP, Best Boy,
and, um, Amy Adams —
O, fierce work of dreaming!

THE HEAVINESS OF A STONE

I never met my father's mother,
he left her there in the old country,
in Bessarabia, between the world wars.

She likely died in the slaughterings.

My mother's mother I know best from
a photograph: a stately woman
in what might have been her wedding dress.

She died when I was four years old.

What can I tell you? In our house
aunts, uncles, back from the graveyard,
first washed hands at the hose on the lawn,
for days *sat shiva* on lowly seats,
orange crates brought from the family store.

I watched them bent low, not understanding.

I was four; I stood in a chair
and wondered to see somehow in the corner
an oval mottled stone, gray-brown,
maybe weighing ten pounds...later learned
the customs of death: that mirrors are draped;
that a stone set down in the house of death
as if the house had swallowed a stone.

THE EDEN STORY

Thinking about the Eden story,
how they had everything nice,
no teenage kids to drive them crazy,
and then along comes spin-doctor snake
with the latest thing, the WANT-device:
"Everyone's doing it, have a taste."

Now here's the part I specially like:
Eve invents the Great Shopping Mantra,
the daily chant of "Gottahaveit!"
and Adam goes along, can't fault
the ladies. Adam's smitten: "Christ,
that's smashing on you" — little black dress —

"why not buy two?"
for she's resplendent
in worldly dazzle. He's saying "Riiiight,"
he's whispering suavely "Go for it, baby."
Eyes closed, mouth open, he nods to her:
"sure, why not, pass us a bite."

WHY WOMEN LOVE GOOD SHOES

A bit because of how they smell
(the craftsman-turn-on, worker in leather)
and more that at first they're painful and yet
comfort comes once "broken-in,"
intimate as tattoos. She cries
"I love my shoes!" the thought of this lowly
reverence involved with high prices, true,
though bargains count as well, they mean
that God had made her a special project...
but price insanely high is best,
a crucial part of the passion, for if
such costly, elegant care is spent
on simple pathetic feet like those
that Jesus washed, how much more flows
toward worthy upwards? She will judge
a man by the state of his heels, by his brand
or shine, but a heel doesn't bother with shine,
he's the sort who'll wear his socks to bed
and smell of work and often complain
that she spends far too much on shoes.

HAPPINESS

is where you stand at noon,
it's right below your feet;
it's the part of you
that doesn't cast a shadow.

HAIRS

A guy years ago in my poetry workshop
went gaga over female hairs
(he would only use the plural, "hairs,"
"a swirl of light on her long curvy hairs").

I brood on that "s," as when Sandra Cisneros
used the jet plane's rest room to dry-rasp
arm-pit "hairs" to meet smooth-shaven
her proper father down Mexico way,

or when Esmeralda Santiago
praised her teacher's "specially beautiful"
legs "because covered
with long thin hairs."

It's fine to praise a women's *hair*
but something other (funny, no?)
to speak of her "hairs." But why? We're told
"He numbereth the hairs on thy head."

There's dignity in that, and consider:
"His eye is on the sparrow," so surely
He must be concerned with you and all your
funky, uncountable hairs.

BITCH-WANTS

I've lived like a greyhound bred to pursue
a dog track's inedible wool-toy rabbit,
teased toward a sense of non-food to tear into,
choked on dead dryness whenever I caught it.

The maze itself was my Minotaur.
Even in loving I'd bang a locked door,
in heaviest weathers raging like Lear —
insane, this fret to be sated, noticed.

Hearth fire, cooking-fire, shouts of the children,
wife's foot pressed against man's hard foot,
these speak to us, though we'd sell our birthright,
trade deep heat for a bargain price-tag,

all the while knowing that joy begins
high in a mountain encampment with friends
or from total work like jogging hard miles
in a dream, no room for anything

but life. Who'll shimmer in coffin-clothes?
And yet bitch-wants demand their kiss
though day in its glory is cloth of gold
and night a bottomless sea.

ALZ

They sear through the mind like falling stars,
these notions that will not stay, so maybe
we're in for some heavy Alz? — names,
concepts, words blink out, oh this
goes beyond mere memory crashes, this
is what-do-they-call-it? *erosion*, whole

weather systems crumble the rock
on which a life was built, odd winds
waltz meanings off and dazed you lumber
after some last flying grains of sense,
no fun for the wife spooning Cream of Wheat
to a flabby puss, plus never again

to make a sale, or flirt with a waitress,
and what will we Alzes dream? *Silent movies.*
Of course. But once those fade to white
what hope for a sequel with A-list casting,
what possible chance for a Hollywood ending
denying the white-out sadness of loss?

PASSENGER WONG

Last courtesy call for Passenger Wong,
his flight to Denver boarding, boarded,
gate about to close, oh Wong
where are you?

And then he appears in a rush at last,
winded, burdened with carry-ons,
a young man whose sneakers are very white.
The courtesy-caller bars his way.

"But I can make it," Wong declares,
seeing his plane within easy reach.
He's sent back to the terminal,
and oh the smirk on the gate-closer's face!

None of us answered Wong's parting question,
none of the processed, on time, waiting:
"Do I have to buy another ticket?"
No, no, dear Wong, we're not *that* vindictive —

I'll speak for us all, uncommiserate then,
who watched you turned away from Denver.
From all of us there in that silent room,
we are sorry, Passenger Wong.

SIXTEEN

I yearned for a girl with rounded heels
no hands-off hands, no unturned pages,

we'd smooth along like hell on wheels...
but what transpired were year-long sieges

for she, she needed a third-eye guy
intelligent down through the muscle

before she'd trade a sigh for a sigh
and let the kettle whistle.

THE JUICE

comes at its richest once denied,
say if you're caught
in a dryland you can't pass through
and it's eight years wide,

or when a face seems just a "this,"
or when your damnable correctitude insists
till nothing in its native self exists —
it's then the juice makes progress.

How do we get cemented in
one corner of the spectrum,
color gone black & white,
stuck at some single sticky end?

Dear passengers in our universe-boat,
comrade sailors, let juices flow,
savor the zest of the billion-paged menu,
for where is it written that you must be

one item? Do it, Genius-Person,
aged and ageless, of multi-hue —
O carry on, kaleidoscopic you!
Let juices flow as they are meant to do!

WALKING WITH THE POET TED MACKER

I'd walk now and then with my young poet friend.
We'd amble over to State Street, down
to the ocean, once saw a shoeless, shirtless
guy handcuffed, four police
to this one shoeless guy,
public profanity the charge.

Often in Ted's poems he's awed
by girls, and when we take our walks
maybe out along State Street Pier,
the girls show up, some display piercings,
midriffs bared, tattoos. Often
these girls smile at Ted, he's a handsome guy.

We'll be chatting, say, about Louis-Ferdinand
Celine when whoa, like a pointer-dog
Ted stops and POINTS: a sighting: my God,
there she is, magnificent She.
We're astonished.
Then we move on.

JOLSON & LOUIE

When I was a kid in Atlantic City
I wowed the old ladies on the beach
with my boy soprano: *My Yiddishe Momme.*
They glowed with affection and Coppertone.

*

Today — believe it — at poetry class,
simply because he'd been mentioned before,
I played some Louie: "Heebie Jeebies,"
"West End Blues," and almost lost it

during that long extended golden
note at the end of "West End" — oh,
it's okay for kids to see teacher weep
when there's genius in the room.

PIANISSIMO

I think of her *pianissimo*,
tilt of her head, slight bloom of a smile,
delicacy, a reverent partaking,
as if she were a slow, bowing pony
grazing tender shoots.

SONG: DESCENDING TO TOUCH

Clouds over mountains gather like lovers.
Descending to touch they melt into mist.

Deer stand still in the old pine forest.
May all the world be safe and blessed.

Descending to touch, melting to mist,
give over stiff-necked posing apart.

May all the world be safe and blessed.
Quiet the brain. Think with the heart.

Give over stiff-necked posing apart.
Deer stand still in the old pine forest.

Wantings cease as healings start.
Clouds over mountains gather like lovers.

Other books from Word Palace Press

How Strange it is to Be Anything at All by Joe Riley
On Tibetan Buddhism, Mantras and Drugs by Allen Ginsberg
Instructions for the Living by Mariko Nagai
Border Songs by Sam Hamill
Under Such Brilliance by Kevin Sullivan
Beauty Like a Rope by Leslie St. John
Wayfaring Stranger by Richard Tillinghast
Who on Earth by Michael Hannon
Celtic Light by Lee Perron
Tilting Point by Peter Dale Scott
Life by Jack Foley
Imaginary Burden by Michael Hannon
A Poem of Miracles by Jerome Rothenberg

Upcoming Titles

Women Under the Influence by Michael Ford

www.ingramcontent.com/pod-product-compliance
Lightning Source LLC
Chambersburg PA
CBHW051704040426
42446CB00009B/1295